The AUSTRALIAN Twelve Days of Christmas

Written and illustrated by
Michael Salmon

First printed 1988

PA-R PRODUCTIONS

Castle Hill
New South Wales 2154
Australia
Reprinted 1989

On the first day of Christmas
my true love sent to me,

A kookaburra in a gum tree.

On the second day of Christmas
my true love sent to me,

Two snakes on skis,

And a kookaburra in a gum tree.

On the third day of Christmas
my true love sent to me,

Three wet galahs,

Two snakes on skis,

And a kookaburra
in a gum tree.

On the fourth day of Christmas
my true love sent to me,

Four lyrebirds,

Three wet galahs,

Two snakes on skis,

And a kookaburra
in a gum tree.

On the fifth day of Christmas
my true love sent to me,

Five kangaroos,

Four lyrebirds,

Three wet galahs,

Two snakes on skis,

And a kookaburra
in a gum tree.

On the sixth day of Christmas
my true love sent to me,

Six sharks a-surfing,

Five
kangaroos,

Four
lyrebirds,

Three
wet galahs,

Two snakes on skis,

And a kookaburra
in a gum tree.

On the seventh day of Christmas
my true love sent to me,

Seven emus laying,

Six sharks
a-surfing,

Five
Kangaroos,

Four
lyrebirds,

Three
wet galahs,

Two
snakes on skis,

And a kookaburra
in a gum tree.

On the eighth day of Christmas
my true love sent to me,

Eight dingos dancing,

Seven
emus laying,

Six
sharks a-surfing,

Five
kangaroos,

Four lyrebirds,

Three wet galahs,

Two snakes on skis,

And a kookaburra
in a gum tree.

On the ninth day of Christmas
my true love sent to me,

Nine crocs a-snoozing?

Eight
dingos dancing,

Seven
emus laying,

Six sharks
a-surfing,

Five
kangaroos,

Four
lyrebirds,

Three
wet galahs,

Two snakes on skis,

And a kookaburra
in a gum tree.

On the tenth day of Christmas
my true love sent to me,

Ten wombats washing,

Nine crocs
a-snoozing?

Eight
dingos dancing,

Seven
emus laying,

Six sharks
a-surfing,

Five
kangaroos,

Four
lyrebirds,

Three
wet galahs,

Two snakes
on skis,

And a
kookaburra
in a gum tree.

On the eleventh day of Christmas
my true love sent to me,

Eleven lizards leaping,

Ten wombats
washing,

Nine crocs
a-snoozing?

Eight
dingos dancing,

Seven
emus laying,

Six sharks
a-surfing,

Five
kangaroos,

Four
lyrebirds,

Three
wet galahs,

Two snakes
on skis,

And a
kookaburra
in a gum tree.

On the twelfth day of Christmas
my true love sent to me,

Twelve possums playing,

Eleven
lizards leaping,

Ten wombats
washing,

Nine crocs
a-snoozing?

Eight dingos
dancing,

Seven
emus laying,

Six sharks
a-surfing,

Five
kangaroos,

Four
lyrebirds,

Three
wet galahs,

Two snakes
on skis,

And a
kookaburra
in a gum tree.

On the twelfth day of Christmas
my true love sent to me,

Twelve
possums playing,

Eleven
lizards leaping,

Ten wombats
washing,

Six sharks
a-surfing,

Five
kangaroos,

Four
lyrebirds,

Nine crocs
a-snoozing?

Eight
dingos dancing,

Seven
emus laying,

Three
wet galahs,

Two
snakes on skis,

And a kookaburra
in a gum tree.

Christmas Eve

Dear Santa
Please fill
up with Lots
of Toys
Dear Santa
here are some
Lamingtons
and milk for
you...

Christmas Day

Boxing Day